Marjoleine's
3D Greetings Cards

Marjolein Zweed

FORTE PUBLISHERS

Contents

© 2003 Forte Uitgevers, Utrecht
© 2003 for the translation by the
publisher
Original title: *Marjoleine's wenskaarten*

ISBN 90 5877 361 2
NUR 475

This is a publication from
Forte Uitgevers BV
P.O. Box 1394
3500 BJ Utrecht
The Netherlands

For more information about the creative
books available from Forte Uitgevers:
www.hobby-party.com

Publisher: Marianne Perlot
Editor: Hanny Vlaar
Photography and digital image editing:
Fotografie Gerhard Witteveen,
Apeldoorn, the Netherlands
Cover and inner design: BADE creatieve
communicatie, Baarn, the Netherlands
Translation: TextCase, Groningen,
the Netherlands

Preface

A couple of years ago, I started designing 3D cutting sheets.

The collection grew and I was often asked whether there was a book

about them. Marianne Perlot gave me the opportunity to write this

book. I designed new 3D cutting sheets and looked for attractive colour

combinations of cards. I also designed a series of pattern sheets which

combine excellently with my 3D cutting sheets. The result is a collection of

new cards with many squares, subtle borders and ton-sur-ton colours.

The results are shown in this book.

Good luck with the cards.

Marjolein

All the examples shown in this book can be found in

my shop **Marjolein Zweed Creatief** in Abbekerk, the Netherlands.

Techniques

Card

Frames made from different coloured card are used for the cards in this book. Subtle borders are created by using pieces of card of slightly different sizes. Always carefully select the right colour of card. The right colour combinations and the pictures are what make the cards attractive.

Ruler

The card can best be cut using a ruler. Be accurate, because that gives the best result. I prefer to use a transparent cutting ruler (Securit). Always cut along the ruler's metal strip. In order to measure the correct dimensions, you can use a cutting mat which has a centimetre scale and the transparent ruler. The 0.5 cm wide blocks which are printed on the ruler are very useful when used in combination with the cutting mat.

Photo glue

It is best to stick the pieces of card together using photo glue, because traces of photo glue can be easily rubbed from the card.

3D pictures

All the cards in this book have 3D pictures. These are made by sticking different layers of the same picture on top of each other. By placing 3D glue or 3D foam tape between the layers, you create depth and the card becomes three-dimensional. The cards in this book have been made using two, three or four layers. You need as many 3D cutting sheets as layers you wish to use. The number of layers used for the cards is stated in each chapter. The cutting patterns used are shown in most of the chapters. Of course, you can always use more or less layers if you wish. Be careful when cutting. The pictures on the cutting sheet are indifferent sizes and some are mirror images. I usually use a knife to cut the straight side of the pictures.

The first (bottom) layer is usually the whole picture. The background is cut away for the second layer. The third and possibly forth layer consist of the bits of the picture which are in the foreground. I usually stick the first layer on the card using photo glue. You can use 3D glue or 3D foam tape for the other layers. Try and find out what you prefer, because this is often a personal choice. Before you stick down the pictures, you can puff them up a bit with your fingers, if you wish.

1. Marjoleine's 3D cutting sheets.

2. Removing the sticker from the sticker sheet.

3. Sticking the sticker on the card.

4. Making the card 3D.

If you use 3D glue, it is best to put it in a syringe so that it is easier to apply. Apply small drops of 3D glue to the back of the picture and carefully stick the picture on top of the previous picture. Do not press too hard, otherwise you will loose the depth. Do the same for the other layers. You must allow the glue to dry properly before posting the card. You can cut 3D foam tape into small pieces and then stick them on the back of the picture. Carefully stick the picture on top of the previous picture. Make sure you stick it in the right place, because you will not be able to slide it about once you have stuck it down. Do the same for the other layers.

Using stickers

You can use napkin tape to help you to stick the stickers in the right place. Napkin tape is blue adhesive tape which is less adhesive than normal tape. (If the tape is still too sticky, you can first press it on your clothes to reduce the adhesive strength.) Stick the tape over the sticker you wish to use and press it down firmly with your nail or the handle of a pair of scissors.

Next, carefully remove the tape from the sticker sheet making sure the sticker comes with it (see step 2, page 5). Stick the tape and the sticker in the correct place on the card and press it down firmly with your nail or the handle of a pair of scissors. Next, carefully remove the tape making sure the sticker stays in place (see step 3, page 5).

You can remove the bits which remain between the letters with the point of a knife.

Materials

- *3D scissors*
  Use a pair of tweezer scissors if you do not like using the 3D scissors.

- *Knife*
  Change your blade regularly to get the best result.

- *Cutting mat*
  Use a cutting mat with a centimetre scale to help you cut the card to the right size.

- *Transparent cutting ruler (Securit)*
  Always cut along the ruler's metal strip. The 0.5 cm wide blocks which are printed on the ruler are very useful when used in combination with the cutting mat.

- *Photo glue*
  If you use photo glue, you can easily remove any traces of glue which are left on the card.

- *3D glue and a syringe*
  If you use 3D glue, it is best to put it in a syringe so that it is easier to apply.

- *3D foam tape*
  Make sure you stick the picture in the right place, because you will not be able to slide it about once you have stuck it down.

- *Marjoleine's 3D cutting sheets*
  Each sheet consists of different squares in a number of different sizes. The sheets are all in one colour and one theme, so that the pictures on one sheet combine nicely together.

- *Marjoleine's pattern sheets*
  This series of pattern sheets combines very nicely with Marjoleine's 3D cutting sheets. The sheets consist of two matching patterns.

- *Papicolor card*
  You can use this card to make your own cards. You can also buy standard and square pre-cut and pre-folded cards. The colour numbers are stated in each chapter.

The other materials are listed in the chapters in which they are used.

Grape hyacinths

The delicate grape hyacinths combine very nicely with the fragile vellum. The beautiful blue colours make the cards complete.

Spring is in the air!

What you need
- ❏ *3D cutting sheet: grape hyacinths (2 or 3 lay ers)*
- ❏ *Papicolor card: iris blue (31) andviolet (20)*
- ❏ *Papicolor paper: violet (20)*
- ❏ *Congratulations vellum: white*
- ❏ *Silhouette punch (107)*
- ❏ *Text sticker: DD1411 silver (Doodey)*

3D pictures
The first layer is the whole picture. The background is cut away for the second layer. Card 4 has a third layer which consists of the grape hyacinths without the stems.

Card 1
Take a standard, iris blue double card (10.5 x 15 cm). Stick a violet rectangle (8.5 x 13 cm) and an iris blue rectangle (8 x 12.5 cm) on this

card. Stick two pictures of grape hyacinths (middle size) on the top card and make them 3D. Finally, stick a text sticker on the card.

Card 2
Take a standard, iris blue double card (10.5 x 15 cm). Fold a strip of vellum (21 x 15 cm) around the card, but do not stick it in place. Stick a strip of iris blue card (4.5 x 15 cm) on the vellum, 1 cm from the right-hand side of the card. Stick a strip of violet card (4 x 15 cm) on top of the iris blue card. Now stick the vellum on the card by only applying glue to the back of the vellum which is hidden by the strips of card. If you

1.

2.

3.

4.

5.

want, you can stick the vellum to the back of the card using a small amount of glue. Stick four pictures of grape hyacinths (smallest size) on the strip and make them 3D.

Card 3

Take a square, violet double card (13 x 13 cm). Stick a piece of iris blue card (10 x 10 cm) on this card. Punch five mosaics out of the paper and then cut each mosaic out as a square (3 x 3 cm). Stick the mosaics and four pictures of grape hyacinths (smallest size) on the card and make the pictures 3D.

Card 4

Take a standard, iris blue double card (10.5 x 15 cm). Fold a strip of vellum (21 x 15 cm) around the card, but do not stick it in place. Stick a piece of iris blue card

(6.5 x 6.5 cm) on the vellum. Now stick the vellum to the card by only applying glue to the back of the vellum which is hidden by the piece of card. The vellum can also be stuck to the back of the card using a small amount of glue. Stick a picture of grape hyacinths (largest size) on the top card and make it 3D.

Card 5

Take a square, iris blue double card (13 x 13 cm). Stick a piece of violet card (10.5 x 10.5 cm) and a piece of iris blue card (10 x 10 cm) on

this card. Stick four pictures of grape hyacinths (middle size) on the top card and make them 3D.

Flowers

My favourite cutting sheet is the one with the white flowers. I love the colour, the roses, the tulips and the memories.

What you need
- ❏ *3D cutting sheets: white flowers (3 layers) and pink flowers (2 layers)*
- ❏ *Pattern sheet: pattern no. 1*
- ❏ *Papicolor card: light green (47), olive green (45), cerise (33) and carnation white (03)*
- ❏ *Gold card*
- ❏ *Vellum: rose with text*
- ❏ *Transparent sticker: gold square (3101)*
- ❏ *Text sticker: DD1411 gold (Doodey)*
- ❏ *Spirelli circle: cream*
- ❏ *Pink thread (Madeira 13)*
- ❏ *Napkin tape*

Card 1

Cut a square (21 x 21 cm) from light green card and fold it double. Stick an olive green strip of card (6.5 x 16.5 cm) and a strip of pattern sheet (6 x 16 cm) on the card. Stick three pictures of white flowers on top (middle size). Stick the transparent stickers over the pictures and then make the pictures 3D.

Card 2
Take a standard, light green double card (10.5 x 15 cm). Fold a strip of pattern sheet (15 x 21 cm) double and stick it around the card. Stick a strip of olive green card (4.5 x 15 cm) 1 cm from the bottom of the card. Stick a strip of light green card (4 x 15 cm) on top of this. Stick four pictures of white flowers (smallest size) on the strip and make them 3D.

Card 3
Take a square, olive green double card (13 x 13 cm). Stick the text around the card (look at the Step-by-step photographs on page 5 and carefully read the instructions given below). Stick napkin tape on the word Many on the-

sticker sheet, so that the edge of the tape is equal with the bottom edge of the word. Next, stick a piece of the tape against the side of the card (see step 2), so that you know where the letter M begins. Stick the edge of the piece of tape with the text sticker against the top of the card. Next, remove the blue tape. Do the same for the word Congratulations, but start working from the right-hand side of the card. Do all four sides of the card in the same way. Stick a piece of gold card (6.5 x 6.5 cm) in the middle of the card. Stick a picture of a white rose (largest size) on top and make it 3D.

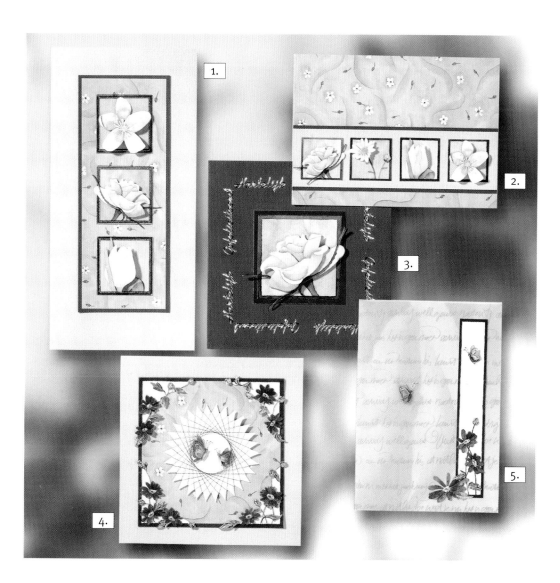

Card 4

Take a square, light green double card (13 x 13 cm). Stick a piece of cerise card (10.5 x 10.5 cm) on this card. Stick a piece of pattern sheet (10 x 10 cm) on top. Stick the large corners of the pink flowers on the pattern sheet so that the corners make one continuous border. Make the corners 3D. Take a Spirelli circle and use adhesive tape to stick the pink thread to the rear of the card. Wind the thread to the front of the card and then to the back again, skipping

ten points. Wind the thread nine points back in the other direction and then to the front of the card again. Skip another ten points and continue all the way round the circle in

the same way. Use adhesive tape to stick the thread to the back of the card. Stick the Spirelli circle on the card. Stick two butterflies on top and make them 3D.

Card 5

Take a standard, carnation white double card (10.5 x 15 cm). Fold a strip of vellum (21 x 15 cm) around the card, but do not stick it in place. Stick the long picture with pink flowers, a butterfly and another pink flower (largest size) on the vellum. Now stick the vellum to the card by only applying glue to the back of the vellum where it is hidden by the pictures. The vellum can also be stuck to the back of the card using a small amount of glue. Make the pictures 3D.

Brown roses

Brown is not the most obvious colour for roses. However, when combined with the correct colour card, the card becomes something special.

What you need
- ❏ *3D cutting sheet: brown roses (4 layers)*
- ❏ *Papicolor card:*
  nut brown (39)
  and dark brown (38)
- ❏ *Papicolor Structura:*
  sand (193)
- ❏ *Lacé duo-colour card:*
  cream/gold
- ❏ *Gold card*
- ❏ *Transparent sticker:*
  gold square (3101)
- ❏ *Lacé template no. 2*
- ❏ *Napkin tape*

Card 1

Cut a strip from the Structura sand card (21 x 15 cm) and fold it double to make a double card (10.5 x 15 cm). Stick a strip of dark brown card (4.5 x 15 cm) 1 cm from the bottom of the card. Stick a strip of Structura sand card (4 x 15 cm) on top of this. Stick four pictures of brown roses (smallest size) on the strip and make them 3D.

Card 2

Take a square, nut brown double card (13 x 13 cm). Stick a piece of dark brown card (10.5 x 10.5 cm) and a piece of Structura sand card (10 x 10 cm) on this card. Stick four pictures of brown roses (second smallest size) on top. Stick the transparent stickers over the pictures and then make the pictures 3D.

Card 3

Cut a strip from the Structura sand card (26 x 13 cm) and fold it double to make a square double card (13 x 13 cm). Stick the large picture of the brown rose in bud on the card and make it 3D.

Card 4

Take a standard, nut brown double card (10.5 x 15 cm). Stick a dark brown piece of card (8 x 8 cm) and a piece of Structura sand card (7.5 x 7.5 cm) on the card. Stick the second largest picture of the open brown rose on the card and make it 3D.

Card 5

Cut a strip (21 x 15 cm) from the Lacé duo-colour card and fold it double to make a double card (10.5 x 15 cm). Strip a strip of dark brown card (4 x 15 cm) 1 cm from the right-hand side of the card. Cut a strip from the duo-colour card (3.5 x 15 cm). Use napkin tape to stick the Lacé template to the gold side of the duo-colour card. Cut all the grooves of the template into the card and remove the template. Score the fold lines at the rear (gold side) of the duo-colour card. Fold every other point forwards and slide them under the points which are not folded forwards. Stick the strip with the Lacé pattern on the strip of dark brown card. Cut three squares (3.5 x 3.5 cm) from the gold card and stick them on the card. Stick three brown roses (smallest size) on the gold squares.

1.

2.

3.

4.

5.

Teddy bears

What is nicer to give to
a new-born baby or a
cute toddler than these
teddy bears?

What you need
- ❏ *3D cutting sheets: pink teddy bears(4 layers)*
  and blue teddy bears (4 layers)
- ❏ *Pattern sheets: pattern no. 7 and pattern no. 8*
- ❏ *Papicolor card:*
  pale pink (23), cerise (33),
  nut brown (39), dark brown (38),
  lavender (21), night blue (41) and
  caramel (26)
- ❏ *Punched out baby's feeding bottle (Sizzix)*
- ❏ *Silhouette template: new baby*
- ❏ *Napkin tape*
- ❏ *Relief gloss*
- ❏ *Cocktail stick*

You can make beady eyes by putting a drop of
relief gloss on a cocktail stick and then dabbing
it on the eyes.

Card 1

Take a standard, pale pink double card (10.5 x 15 cm). Fold a strip of pattern sheet (no. 8, 15 x 21 cm) double and stick it around the card. Stick a piece of cerise card (6 x 10.5 cm) and a piece of pattern sheet (no. 8, 5.5 x 10 cm) on the card. Stick two pictures of two bears (middle size) from the pink teddy bear sheet on top and make them 3D.

Card 2

Cut a square (21 x 21 cm) from nut brown card and fold it double. Stick a strip of dark brown card (9 x 19.5 cm) and a strip of pattern sheet (no. 7, 8.5 x 19 cm) on the card. Stick the large strip from the blue teddy bear sheet on top and make it 3D.

Card 3

Take a standard, nut brown double card (10.5 x 15 cm). Stick a piece of pattern sheet (no. 7, 9.5 x 14 cm) on top. Stick the picture of the five teddy bears on top and make it 3D.

Card 4

Take a square, lavender double card
(13 x 13 cm). Stick a piece of night blue card
(10 x 10 cm) on this card. Stick a piece of pattern
sheet (no. 7, 9.5 x 9.5 cm) on top. Stick the
large picture of the elephant and the dog from
the blue teddy bear sheet on top and make it 3D.

Card 5

Take a standard, pale pink double card
(10.5 x 15 cm). Fold a strip of pattern sheet
(no. 8, 15 x 21 cm) double and stick it around
card. Stick the large picture of the two bears
from the pink teddy bear sheet on top and
make it 3D.

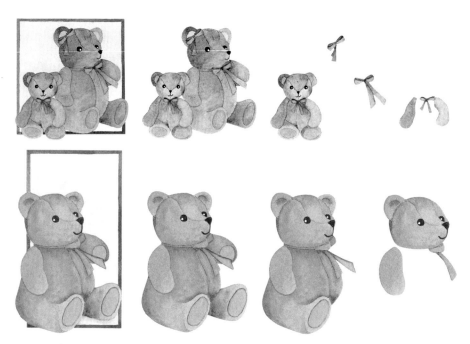

1.

2.

3.

4.

5.

6.

7.

8.

Card 6

Take a standard, lavender double card (10.5 x 15 cm). Fold a strip of pattern sheet (no. 7, 15 x 21 cm) double and stick it around the card. Stick the picture of the bear from the blue teddy bear sheet on top and make it 3D.

Card 7

Take a square, nut brown double card (13 x 13 cm). Stick a piece of caramel card (10 x 10 cm) on this card. Use napkin tape to stick the silhouette template to a piece of nut brown card. Cut the shapes of the safety pins and the dummy out of the card. Remove the template. Cut a square (4.5 x 4.5 cm) around the safety pins and the dummy. Stick the cut out shapes on the pattern sheet (no. 7) and cut

them out. Stick them on the card. Stick two more nut brown squares (4.5 x 4.5 cm) on the card and stick a piece of pattern sheet (no. 7, 4 x 4 cm) on each of these squares. Use 3D glue or 3D foam tape to stick a rabbit and a sheep from the pink teddy bear sheet on each square.

Card 8

Take a square, pale pink double card (13 x 13 cm). Stick a piece of cerise card (10.5 x 10.5 cm) on this card. Stick a piece of pattern sheet (no. 8, 10 x 10 cm) on top. Use the Sizzix die cutter to cut a baby's feeding bottle from cerise card and stick this on the pattern sheet using 3D glue or 3D foam tape. Stick the bear from the pink teddy bear sheet against the bottle using 3D glue or 3D foam tape and make it 3D.

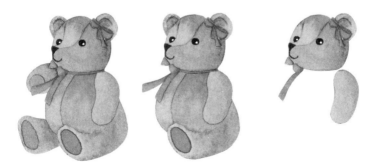

Pink roses

Pink roses for Mother's Day,

Valentine's Day, your

grandmother's birthday or just

to let someone know how much

you care.

What you need
- ❏ *3D cutting sheet: pink roses (4 layers)*
- ❏ *Pattern sheet: pattern no. 8*
- ❏ *Papicolor card: pale pink (23)*
  and cerise (33)
- ❏ *Papicolor paper: cerise (33)*
- ❏ *Border ornament punch: diamond*
- ❏ *Number punch: 5, 0 with holder*

(no. 8, 15 x 21 cm) and punch a pattern in the short side (start in the middle). Next, stick the pale pink strip on the inside of the card and the pattern sheet on the outside of the card so that the holes are slightly staggered. Cut the pattern sheet level with the left-hand side of the card so that it does not protrude. Stick the picture of the pink rose in bud (middle size) on the card and make the rose 3D. Punch the 5 and the 0 out of cerise paper and stick them on the card.

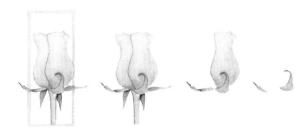

Card 1
Take a standard, cerise double card (10.5 x 15 cm). Use the border ornament punch to punch out the right-hand border of the card (start in the middle). Take a strip of pale pink card (2.5 x 15 cm) and punch a pattern in it (start in the middle). Take a strip of pattern sheet

Card 2
Take a standard, pale pink double card (10.5 x 15 cm). Stick a cerise rectangle (9 x 13 cm) and a rectangle from the pattern sheet (8.5 x 13 cm) on this card. Stick three pictures of pink roses in bud (smallest size) on top and make them 3D.

Card 3

Take a square, cerise double card (13 x 13 cm). Stick a piece of the cutting sheet (12.5 x 12.5 cm) on this card and stick a piece of cerise card (8.5 x 8.5 cm) on top. Stick the large open rose on top and make it 3D.

Card 4

Take a standard, pale pink double card (10.5 x 15 cm). Fold a strip of pattern sheet (no. 8, 15 x 21 cm) double and stick it around the card. Stick the large picture of the rose in bud on top and make it 3D. Cut a square (4.3 x 4.3 cm) from cerise card and stick this on the card using 3D glue or foam tape. Stick a picture of an open rose (second smallest size) on top and make it 3D.

Card 5

Cut a square (21 x 21 cm) from pale pink card and fold it double. Stick a strip of cerise card (6.5 x 16.5 cm) and a strip of pattern sheet (6 x 16 cm) on the card. Stick three pictures of roses (second smallest size) on top and make them 3D.

Card 6

Take a square, pale pink double card (13 x 13 cm). Stick a piece of cerise card (8.5 x 8.5 cm) and a piece of the pattern sheet (8 x 8 cm) on this card. Stick four pictures of a rose (smallest size) on the top card and make them 3D.

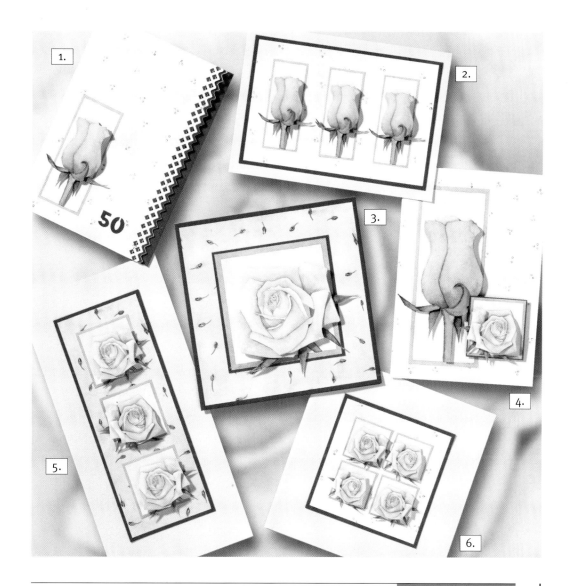

Sunflowers

The warm combination of mustard yellow and denim blue cheers everybody up.

What you need
- ❏ *3D cutting sheets:*
  sunflower (3 layers),
  leaves (3 layers),
  yellow flowers (2 layers) and
  butterflies (2 layers)
- ❏ *Pattern sheets:*
  pattern no. 1, pattern no. 2 and pattern no. 4
- ❏ *Papicolor card:*
  mustard yellow (48),
  cream (27) and nut brown (39)
- ❏ *Papicolor Antica Denim Blue (165)*
- ❏ *Raffia*
- ❏ *Spirelli circle: pale yellow*
- ❏ *Copper thread (Madeira Copper)*
- ❏ *Number punch: 2, 5 with holder*

Card 1

Cut a square (21 x 21 cm) from denim blue card and fold it double. Stick a strip of mustard yellow card (6.5 x 16.5 cm) and a strip of pattern sheet (no. 1, 6 x 16 cm) on the card. Stick three pictures of leaves on top (middle size). The background is cut away for the second layer. The picture with two leaves has a third layer which is the foremost leaf.

Card 2

Take a square, mustard yellow double card (13 x 13 cm). Stick a piece of cream card (9.5 x 9.5 cm) on this card and stick a piece of pattern sheet (no. 2, 9 x 9 cm) on top. Take a Spirelli circle and use adhesive tape to stick the copper thread to the rear of the card. Wind the thread to the front of the card and then to the back again, skipping ten points. Wind the thread nine points back in the other direction and then to the front of the card again. Skip another ten points and continue all the way round the circle in the same way. Use adhesive tape to stick the thread to the back of the card. Stick the Spirelli circle on the card. Stick a butterfly on top and make it 3D.

Card 3

Cut a strip (26 x 13 cm) from the denim blue card and fold it double to make a square double card (13 x 13 cm). Stick a piece of mustard yellow card (10.5 x 10.5 cm) on the card and stick a piece of pattern sheet (no. 4, 10 x 10 cm) on top. Stick a picture of a sunflower (largest size) on the top card and make it 3D. Use raffia to attach a label to the stem of the sunflower.

Card 4

Take a standard, mustard yellow double card (10.5 x 15 cm). Stick a piece of nut brown card (6.5 x 6.5 cm) on the card. Stick the large picture of the gerbera on top and make it 3D. The background has been cut away for the second layer. Stick a butterfly on top and make it 3D.

Card 5

Take a standard, mustard yellow double card (10.5 x 15 cm). Stick a strip of pattern sheet (no. 4, 6 x 13.5 cm) on the left-hand side of the card. Stick the long pictures of the sunflowers on top of this and make them 3D. Use raffia to attach a label to a stem of one of the sunflowers. Cut two large butterflies out of pattern sheet no. 2 and use 3D glue or 3D foam tape to stick them on the card. Punch the 2 and the 5 out of pattern sheet no. 4 and stick them on the card.

Card 6

Take a standard, mustard yellow double card (10.5 x 15 cm). Fold a strip of pattern sheet (no. 2, 15 x 21 cm) double and stick it around the card. Stick a strip of nut brown card

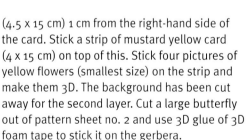

(4.5 x 15 cm) 1 cm from the right-hand side of the card. Stick a strip of mustard yellow card (4 x 15 cm) on top of this. Stick four pictures of yellow flowers (smallest size) on the strip and make them 3D. The background has been cut away for the second layer. Cut a large butterfly out of pattern sheet no. 2 and use 3D glue of 3D foam tape to stick it on the gerbera.

Card 7

Cut a strip (26 x 13 cm) from the denim blue card and fold it double to make a square double card (13 x 13 cm). Stick a piece of mustard yellow card (8.5 x 8.5 cm) and a piece of denim blue card (8 x 8 cm) on the card. Pay attention to the linear direction of the stripes. Stick four pictures of leaves on top (smallest size). The background is cut away for the second layer. The pictures with two leaves have a third layer which is the fore-most leaf.

1.

2.

3.

4.

5.

6.

7.

The beach

The sun on your back, a cool drink and the sea breeze. These cards make you think of long summer days spent on the beach.

What you need
- ❏ *3D cutting sheet: beach (3 layers)*
- ❏ *Papicolor card: night blue (41), lavender (21) and fiesta red (12)*
- ❏ *Silhouette template: boat*
- ❏ *Napkin tape*

Card 1
Take a square, night blue, double card (13 x 13 cm). Stick a piece of fiesta red card

(8.5 x 8.5 cm) and a piece of lavender blue (8 x 8 cm) on this card. Stick two pictures of the boat and two pictures of the seagull (smallest size) on the top card and make them 3D.

Card 2
Take a standard, lavender double card (10.5 x 15 cm). Use napkin tape to stick the silhouette template to the inside of the card. Cut the sailing boat out of the card and remove the template. Take a piece of night blue card (7.5 x 14.5 cm) and cut out a rectangular frame 1 cm from all the sides of the card. Stick this inside the card so that

a frame can be seen on the front of the card. Stick a strip of night blue card (2.5 x 13 cm) on the card next to the boat. Stick the picture of the lighthouse on top and make it 3D.

Card 3

Cut a square (21 x 21 cm) from lavender card and fold it double. Stick a strip of fiesta red card (6.5 x 16.5 cm) and a strip of lavender card

(6 x 16 cm) on the card. Stick three pictures from the beach sheet (middle size) on top and make them 3D.

Card 4

Take a square, lavender double card (13 x 13 cm). Stick the large picture of the cart on top and make it 3D.

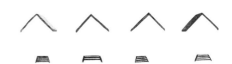

Card 5

Take a standard, night blue double card (10.5 x 15 cm). Stick the picture of the beach cabins on top and make it 3D.

The materials used can be ordered by shopkeepers from: • Kars & Co B.V. in Ochten, the Netherlands • Jalekro B.V. in Assendelft, the Netherlands • Papicolor International B.V. in Utrecht, the Netherlands • Doodey-Double M Decorations in Vlijmen, the Netherlands